LIVING WATERS

CLAIRE ELIZABETH GROSE

Copyright © 2025 by Claire Elizabeth Grose

Compiled and edited by Michael Grose and June Kennedy

All rights reserved. No portion of this publication may be reproduced, stored in a retrieval system or transmitted in any form by any means – electronic, mechanical, photocopying, recording, or any other –except for brief quotation in printed reviews, without the prior written permission of the publisher.

Unless indicated otherwise, all scripture quotations in this book are from the following source:

The Good News Bible: The Bible in Today's English Version (TEV) © 1976 by the American Bible Society. Used with permission.

ISBN 978-0-6459888-4-0

Author contact information - clairegrose.heartmatters@gmail.com

Version 1.0

DEDICATION

This book is dedicated to Jaxon,
My beloved Grandson

CONTENTS

DEDICATION	IV
CONTENTS	V
PREFACE	VIII
ACKNOWLEDGEMENTS	X
PART ONE	1
MY DAILY PRAYER	4
LIVING WATERS	5
ORDAINED BY GOD	6
MY LIFEBUOY	7
STREAMS OF LOVE	8
DIAMOND STARS	9
BELIEVE	10
WORLDS APART LOVE	11
WATERFALL OF BLESSINGS	14
WALKING THROUGH YOUR BEAUTY	15
THANK YOU FOR YOUR BLESSINGS	16
RIPPLES OF JOY	17
THE GLORY OF YOUR BEAUTY	18
LOVING YOU	19
FOLLOW HIS LEAD	20
RIPPLE EFFECT	21
PRAISE HIS HOLY NAME	22
LIVING YOUR WORD	23
RIPPLES OF HIS LOVE	26
BLESSINGS NOT BY CHANCE	27
CALM WATERS	28
A LOVE THAT UNDERSTANDS	29
PART TWO	30
A HOME FOR PRAYER	33
THE POWER OF HIS SPIRIT	34
STILL THE WATERS	35
CHANNEL OF LOVE	36

WHEN YOUR FAITH IS TESTED	37
WAVE HIS BANNER HIGH	38
HEALED BY YOUR BEAUTY	41
UPS AND DOWNS	42
THE RIPPLES OF GOD'S GRACE	43
HOLY SPIRIT'S WHISPERS	44
HEALING WATERS	45
THE SPIRIT'S BALM	46
HIS REASONS	49
KEEPER OF MY SOUL	50
RESTORE ME LORD	51
WASHED BY THE SPIRIT	52
RENEW MY STRENGTH	53
BATHE YOUR SORROWS	54
VICTORY IN THE SPIRIT	57
PRESS INTO THE SAVIOUR	58
REFRESH MY HEART	59
LIFE WEAVES A JOURNEY	60
I CAN'T LIVE WITHOUT YOU	61
GOD'S HELP TODAY	62
AWAKEN MY SPIRIT	63
CALL ON THE SAVIOUR	64
GOD'S PARADISE	65
THANK HIS SPIRIT	66
BORN AGAIN	67
ACKNOWLEDGE GOD	68
PART THREE	69
CALL GOD INTO YOUR LIFE	72
FLOWING STREAMS	73
I PRAY TO YOU LORD	74
BAPTISM OF LOVE	75
BUILD ON YOUR FAITH	76
THE SPIRIT BRINGS YOU NEAR LORD	77
WATERS THAT SPARKLE AND SHINE	80
CALL ON THE SPIRIT	81

- YOUR GREAT MAGNITUDE 82
- RIGHT THE WRONG 83
- ALL THINGS BRAND NEW 84
- A VESSEL FOR JESUS 85

PART FOUR 86
- PROPHECY REVEALED 89
- FATHER OF MANKIND 90
- FILL ME WITH GOODNESS 91
- HE LED BY EXAMPLE 94
- THE SYMBOL OF THE CROSS 95
- FIRST CHRISTMAS MORN 98
- IN AWE SHE HELD HIM 99
- WHAT JOY, WHAT JOY 100
- TRUTH AND GRACE HIS STRONGHOLD 101

PREFACE

Two things I just wanted to say about this book are, why I started writing and how I came by the title.

I grew up in the 1950's-1960's in Adelaide, South Australia, my life was pretty simple but wonderful. I was very lucky to have a secure family life, and my Mum and Dad brought the family up to treat others with respect, do the right thing, be courteous, and respect your elders. We had a strict upbringing and even as adults our parents never criticized us but encouraged us to do our best in life. They were "Aussie battlers" but we always managed to make it through the tough times!

They were people of integrity and cared about others and instilled that into our family.

Church was a big part of our lives growing up. We went to Sunday School at an early age and progressed up through the appropriate groups as we got older.

Youth groups, camps and church anniversaries were all important to the whole family. We competed in church sports teams, basketball and tennis with other parishes across Adelaide. Life-long friendships were in the making and cherished golden memories to look back on that would never fade.

Bible stories, hymns and choruses were all part of getting to know Jesus. This nurturing finally led me to the day Jesus came knocking on my heart's door. Being filled with the Holy Spirit is something I will never forget and the overwhelming power of His love that filled my whole being and propelled me to the front of the hall to give my heart to Him. No words can fully describe the joy I felt. That was in February 1968, I was 14 years of age. He has been my Shining Light ever since, and lives within me always.

So I thank my beautiful Mum and Dad for the way they raised me and for the foundation of knowing Jesus' love.

It was in His love that I started to write, in the Autumn of 1993. My journey has brought me to this book "Living Waters", my 14th book. I was thinking of how the Holy Spirit's power to wash us clean inside comes over us when we believe. Words can not explain the wonder and awe I felt at that time. The change that came over me was surreal and glorious!

I love the scripture verse when Jesus met the Samarian woman at the well and told her about His life-giving water. "If you only knew what God gives and who it is that is asking you for a drink, you would ask him, and he would give you life-giving water."
John 4:10 - Good News Bible.
"...The water that I will give him will become in him a spring which will provide him with life-giving water and give him eternal life."
John 4:14 - Good News Bible.

When I was a young Christian reading my Bible was really important to me in getting to know Jesus as my personal Saviour and became the foundation that I built my faith on.

It gave me strength and courage as I began life in the workforce at the age of 16. Coming from a sheltered upbringing it was my life-line to self-confidence and adapting to social life at work.
The poems reflect the everyday feelings and emotions that we feel as we meet the challenges of life and how the great magnitude of God's love can help us rise above them.

Many of these writings have been my first words of whispered prayer, so much that I have been moved to write them down at once and continue on in His wonderful and absolute love.

Together we write as He provides my inspiration.

All glory to Him, my precious Lord Jesus!

ACKNOWLEDGEMENTS

My heartfelt thanks to my beloved family, my Mum and Dad, Lilly and Ken, and my siblings Jeanette, June, Carol, Gloria and Lynne, for their never ending encouragement and support to me. To the rest of the family, you are all a precious link that joins us together.

To Michael and Andrew for your continual support to me in fulfilling my passion of writing poems for the Lord to help others through His Word.

A huge thank you to Junie for editing my poems and the coffees and lunches we enjoyed along the way.

To Joy Furnell for her Crown of Thorns drawing, you have an amazing gift, thank you Joy.

A special thank you to Salisbury Uniting Church, Adelaide for photos. Used by permission.

A big thank you to Lynne, Jane and Scott, for great photos.

To my friends and Church Families, thank you for your love and support.

To my beautiful sons, Michael and Andrew, and your families. Thank you for loving me, and I am so glad He gave you to me. I cherish my grandchildren, I love you all so much.

To you the reader, thank you for picking this book up and I pray you will find His peace and love on the pages ahead.

May He shower you all with His love and blessings.

PART ONE

"…but whoever drinks the water that I will give him will never be thirsty again. The water that I will give him will become in him a spring which will provide him with life-giving water and give him eternal life."

John 4 : 14

LIVING WATERS

JESUS SAVES…
FEEL REFRESHED, RESTORED…

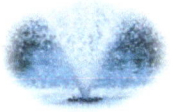

"As fresh water brings joy to the thirsty, so God's people rejoice when He saves them."

Isaiah 12 : 3

MY DAILY PRAYER

Be with me, stay with me,
Close by my side,
Fill me with Your peace and love,
So my spirit shall surely fly
To the heights in Your love,
As only You can give,
Prepare me for this day ahead,
So in me You'll always live.

LIVING WATERS

His living waters heal our hurts
With oil fragrant sweet,
Smoothing out the layers
With His love that's so complete.

His living waters shine like diamonds
In His light of love,
Sparkling every moment
In His realm above.

His living waters you can drink,
You'll never thirst again,
Forever in His Kingdom
If your heart you give to Him.

His living waters come
To wash you clean inside,
A moving of His Spirit
To open your heart wide.

His living waters flow
From His Heavenly Throne,
Where Father and Son abide
To bring you home.

Wonder and awe await
Far beyond your dreams,
Living waters flow for you
From His Throne in crystal streams.

ORDAINED BY GOD

Every believer of the Saviour
Is ordained by God,
They carry His anointing
To pass His message on.

His Spirit lives within
Each heart ordained by God,
An endowment of His ways
For you to act upon.

Many lessons to be learned
As you journey through life,
Ordained by God
You have to shine your light.

Each precious soul
Who receives His mercy and grace,
Has a commitment to reveal
The wonders of trust and faith.

Thank You precious Lord
For speaking the truth,
To each open heart
That's been ordained by You.

Forever and ever
Your Power will remain,
Our Saviour, Lord and God
Blessed is Your Name.

MY LIFEBUOY

My lifebuoy is my Saviour
Ready for my call,
My Counsellor at all times
To whom I surrender my all.

My emotions are tossed about
In rough and turbulent seas,
But my lifebuoy is around me
To give stability.

Though challenges come along,
Sometimes too much to bear,
My lifebuoy never leaves me,
His strength will be there.

He will soothe the waves
And hush the raging wind,
Peace and calm will come
That the heart will feel within.

My lifebuoy can withstand
The deepest, darkest storm,
His outstretched hand is reaching
To open the coming dawn.

Receive Him as your lifebuoy,
Eternal Saviour, King of Kings,
Take His gift of life
Because you are His everything!

STREAMS OF LOVE

Streams of love come down
From Your heavenly Throne,
Cascading like a waterfall
Into hearts that are Your home.

Like the sunrays at dusk
Reach from the heavens above,
Reflecting Your shining light
That shows Your glorious love.

Streams of love so precious
To every challenge we see,
Give strength and healing goodness,
Believe you will receive.

We only have to ask
The Saviour into our heart,
We will receive these streams of love
That will flow over our path.

His streams of love are life changing
When you believe He is the Risen Lord,
He will flood your heart with His Spirit,
So, you can live in one accord.

DIAMOND STARS

Diamond stars ride the crest
Of ripples to the shore
By the ebb of the tide,
A wonder I adore.

So many you could never count,
They shine everywhere,
Diamond stars ride the crests,
What joy I have to share.

Diamond stars on ripples,
Sun shining on the sea
Brings such healing and wonder
To the soul in me.

Surely such beauty
From the Lord above,
Diamond stars on ripples
Bring His wonder and love.

Diamond stars capture my heart,
Mother Nature shining bright,
Diamond stars on ripples
Such a glorious sight.

BELIEVE

The splendour of Your love Lord
Spreads into Eternity,
It overflows in the hearts
Of those who believe.

A simple act of inviting
The Lord into your heart,
"Come into my heart today"
Is all you have to ask.

No power on earth can reveal this love,
It comes from the Trinity,
Believe in the power of His Name,
His blessings you will receive.

The gift of the Spirit
Shows in simplicity,
The love of the Saviour,
Who leads us to believe.

Such a precious gift
To last all time,
When you believe He died upon the Cross
And rose to everlasting life.

Our precious Lord Jesus
In all His Majesty,
Holds a Crown of Life
For all who believe.

WORLDS APART LOVE

Worlds apart love
Came from Eternity,
A realm far beyond earth
To set our soul free.

A love brought to earth
By the Saviour alone,
He brought light to the world
So our heart He could own.

Worlds apart love
Comes with pure joy divine,
No other love like it
He will make your soul shine.

A heavenly endowment
Into your soul,
Where Christ lives
Through the Spirit to make you whole.

Worlds apart love
Will surely bring
A Crown of Life to you
When you open your heart to Him.

LIVING WATERS

HIS BLESSINGS WILL COME …
AS A SURPRISE…

"Out of the fullness of his grace he has blessed
us all, giving us one blessing after another."

John 1 : 16

WATERFALL OF BLESSINGS

A waterfall of blessings
Will cascade over you,
When you commit to the Saviour
He will help you, this is true.

He will open your heart
And fill it to the brim,
With blessings so special
Because they come from Him.

They will flow like a waterfall
To refresh and renew,
Some will sparkle
Like the morning dew.

God's waterfall of blessings
Will lift you to the heights,
As you wear His name
The Lord you can glorify.

His waterfall of blessings
You can claim them every day,
From your giving heart
You can pass them on today.

WALKING THROUGH YOUR BEAUTY

Walking through Your beauty Lord
Brings joy to me,
Your glorious creation
Is what I see.

Your trees and parks,
Valleys and hills,
Such peace and calm
Is what I feel.

Walking through Your beauty Lord,
Past lakes and rocky streams,
A bounty of beauty
Is what I see.

Even the deserts
Dry with sand,
Every ridge formed
By Your Holy hand.

Walking through Your beauty Lord,
My favourite time of all,
When golden leaves float to earth
As Autumn gives the call.

THANK YOU FOR YOUR BLESSINGS

Thank You for Your blessings Lord
That You pour on me each day,
In quiet prayer I ask
That You will share my day.

I don't see them coming
But when they arrive,
Such a special endowment
Upon my daily life.

Whether they are big or small
Each one will surely shine,
As they make their way
Into this heart of mine.

Thank You for Your blessings Lord
That lift any day,
Help me to recognize each one
As they come my way.

RIPPLES OF JOY

Ripples of joy flow from the heart
When you surrender to the Lord,
Holy Spirit comes to live within,
A revelation to adore.

The journey never stops
Of reaching out
To bless a friend
Feeling fear or doubt.

Sharing a care through ripples of joy
Reflect divine, holy love,
Through His Holy Spirit
Who came down from above.

Ripples of joy
Are full of light,
His glory will be shown
For the challenges of life.

Ripples of joy straight from His Throne
Come to you in streams of light,
The wonders of the Saviour
To make your life so bright.

THE GLORY OF YOUR BEAUTY

The glory of Your beauty Lord
Touches my soul,
The glory of Your beauty
Makes me whole.

Your Creation and Your beauty Lord
Refreshes my day,
Because in sight and smell,
I see what You made.

I pray mankind will stop
To notice Thee,
The glory of Your beauty Lord
Speaks so loud to me.

From the smallest grain of sand
To the tallest mountain peak,
Ocean depths and forest glades
Bring Your beauty to me.

The glory of Your beauty Lord,
A wonder to me,
The glory of Your beauty Lord,
I want the world to see.

LOVING YOU

Loving You I must
Every day call You close,
Loving You my Saviour
My eternal Heavenly Host.

You, my precious Saviour
Are love itself,
Flamed by the Spirit
To make Your presence felt.

Loving You I know,
You came to me
Through Your Holy Spirit,
He led me to believe.

Your love makes me love
Because Your Spirit lives within,
Your presence I feel
Because He truly gives.

In loving You Holy Father
The Spirit is my guide,
In loving You Prince of Peace
You are always by my side.

FOLLOW HIS LEAD

Follow the Saviour's lead,
The Redeemer of the world,
His commands are forever,
His message we must tell.

His gift of salvation
For all mankind,
Is ours for the taking
When in His ways we abide.

The beckoning of His Spirit
So real and so pure,
A call you must answer,
Eternal life secure.

Follow His lead in His Word,
Such comfort and peace evermore,
Words pouring from His Thorne
Like a graceful waterfall.

RIPPLE EFFECT

A ripple effect on your heart,
That's what God's love will do
In the state of devotion,
Others will see it too.

This ripple effect
Is one you cannot stop,
By the Spirit's power
It will surge along.

This ripple effect
You may not understand,
His tender gentle love
Will move as He has planned.

Yes, reaching out in gentle pools
To turn your life around,
The ripple effect of God's love,
No greater gift is found.

This ripple effect
Powered by God,
Forever reaching out
Will never, ever stop.

PRAISE HIS HOLY NAME

Praise His Holy Name,
Jesus Christ the Lord,
The glorious King of Kings,
The Messiah of all.

Praise His Holy Name
In all circumstances of life,
To God we are all equal
And precious in His sight.

Praise His Holy Name,
The Name above all Names,
Especially when you pray,
Pray in His Name.

His heavenly Hosts sing praises,
Praises to the Lord,
Almighty Son of God,
You; We must adore.

LIVING YOUR WORD

Your living Word so vital
To our daily lives,
When we consult You Lord
You are by our side.

When we come to a decision
To live by Your Word,
The Spirit will help us,
His prompts are heard.

A need will come to us
More powerful than anything,
A passion to obey
And serve our heavenly King.

Yes, living Your Word Lord
Is a commitment every day,
A love we just can't stop
Will show us the way.

LIVING WATERS

HIS MESSAGE SPREADS…
LIKE RIPPLES IN A POOL…

"From the sky you send rain on the hills,
and the earth is filled with your blessings."

Psalm 104 : 13

RIPPLES OF HIS LOVE

Ripples of His love
Spread far and wide,
An ebb that keeps on moving
Just like the ceaseless tide.

A fragrance sweet and pure
You just can't resist,
Will come from the ripples
Like the morning mist.

The ripples of His love
Will permeate the earth,
Touching open hearts
That are ready to serve.

Quietly and gently
Hearts will realise,
The moving of His Spirit
Cannot be denied.

Nothing can stop this motion,
Obedience is the key,
The ripples of God's love
Will bring you to your knees.

The jubilation in Heaven
As waves of angels roar
When each soul is saved,
It's you He just adores!

BLESSINGS NOT BY CHANCE

Daily blessings come quietly
We don't even know,
Sometimes not recognised
But from God they flow.

We think "how did that happen",
Or why? We may ask,
The Saviour sends each one
Indeed not by chance.

Every blessing comes from Heaven
In many different ways,
A surprise to each heart
On those special days.

Blessings have a purpose
Rich in every way,
No earthly prize can match
What God sends every day.

Blessings not by chance
Are the wonder of His love,
Beyond our understanding
To show how much we're loved.

CALM WATERS

Look for calm waters
In your daily life,
Ask the Saviour every day
To be your shining light.

He can smooth your path ahead
If you ask in His Name,
He will help you jump shadows,
And protect you through driving rain.

Look for calm waters
By calling on His Name,
He will never leave you,
He comes with His mercy and grace.

Look for calm waters,
Your soul needs it so,
You can keep a happy heart
And let your troubles go.

Seek the calm waters
That the Lord walked upon,
His wings will come for shelter
That you can ride upon.

A LOVE THAT UNDERSTANDS

A love that claims you
Will never let you go,
Ever passing through you
In a steady flow.

It will sustain you
And build your strength,
Relying on the Saviour
Will change the way you think.

A love that forgives
When you fail to obey,
A love that has no end
If you lose your way.

A love that understands
Everything you do,
A love that never fails
Is His love that changes you.

PART TWO

"I will make rivers flow among barren hills and springs of water run in the valleys. I will turn the desert into pools of water and the dry land into flowing springs."

Isaiah 41 : 18

HIS LOVE FLOWS...
LIKE A RIVER...

"There is a river that brings joy to the city of God,
to the sacred house of the Most High."

Psalm 46 : 4

A HOME FOR PRAYER

A request from my heart
Rests on trust and faith,
On it's way to heaven's realm
Where it will find its place.

A place of its own Lord
Where You will decide its home,
According to Your will
It will have a "yes "or "no".

My faithful heart will accept
The outcome you decide,
I will use my trust in You
Though it may take some time.

I see it as a lesson
Whatever it may be,
So thank You Holy Father
For always guiding me.

There's always a home for prayer
In the Father's hands,
His decision is final,
His Word is His command.

THE POWER OF HIS SPIRIT

The power of His Spirit
Lays deep inside,
To every welcoming soul
Who opens their heart wide.

His Spirit so special
Lives in open hearts,
He reveals to you so clearly
The passion of your path.

Doubts and fears that hurt you,
You can hand to Him,
Claim His help every day,
His love will never dim.

His peace will come upon you
To lift your heart so high,
The power of His Spirit
Will bring tears to your eyes.

The power of His Spirit
Comes with balm to heal,
Pray for His help today
His strength you will feel.

STILL THE WATERS

When life seems to cast a shadow,
Seek the Saviour's arms,
Still the waters inside you,
Pray for peace and calm.

The Holy Spirit's love
Will come to comfort and heal,
He can still the waters,
His presence is so real.

He calls for humility
In the race of each day,
Keep the peace in all things,
He will show you the way.

Still the waters around you
By praying to rise above
These challenges in life,
The Spirit will come.

Still the waters around you,
Surrender to the King of Kings,
Let this battle go
So His healing can begin.

CHANNEL OF LOVE

He bids you enter
Through His channel of love,
A home of peace
That He sends from above.

His channel of love
A harbour of peace,
For you to go to
And receive His mighty strength.

His channel of love
Will serve you well,
It will endure forever,
As His Word tells.

It's open to all who will come
From wherever you are,
His channel of love is open,
You can come as you are.

Crystal waters so calm
Will refresh your life,
So you can reflect
On His glorious shining light.

His Spirit is the beacon to guide you
Through the shallows of life,
His channel of love is longing
To guide you through day and night.

WHEN YOUR FAITH IS TESTED

When your faith is tested
God stands close to you,
Though you think He's distant,
He's right beside you.

You may feel all alone
And have no drive to act,
That's when His Holy Spirit
Comes to bring you back.

You can never fall
Too far from His arms,
They can always reach you
To restore your peace and calm.

When your faith is tested
And you have doubts and fears,
Open His Word,
It will draw Him near.

When your faith is tested,
Victory you can claim,
Because you are His child
You don't have to carry shame.

You can rise to victory
Over challenges in life,
When your faith is tested
He's right by your side.

WAVE HIS BANNER HIGH

Wave His banner high
When shadows fall,
There's no one else
To help you stand tall.

Though doubts creep in,
Stand firm in God's love,
His grace is sufficient
To raise you high above.

Wave His banner high
To His glory above,
Keep your trust and faith
Firm in His love.

He will see your witness
As you wave His banner high,
He's storing your rewards
You will receive in His time.

CLAIM JESUS…
YOUR HARBOUR OF PEACE…

"On each bank of the stream all kinds of trees will grow to provide food. Their leaves will never wither, and they will never stop bearing fruit."

Ezekiel 47 : 12

HEALED BY YOUR BEAUTY

I'm being healed by Your beauty
Everlasting Lord,
Your beauty that surrounds me
Makes me love You even more.

You send Your healing Spirit
To watch over me,
Wherever I am
That's where You will be.

I'm healed by Your beauty
In majestic soaring trees,
Fields of crops and poppies
And the ebb of the sea.

A dawn that strikes the sky
In flaming orange and red,
Pastels in the clouds
As the sun slowly sets.

I'm healed by Your beauty Lord,
My soul tells me so,
Because You live within me
That's how I know.

UPS AND DOWNS

Life is full of ups and downs
But the downs are lessons learnt,
They make the heart grow stronger
Because happiness we yearn.

The ups make our light shine bright
Nurtured by the Spirit within,
He prompts us with His knowledge
Of how we should live.

Some days there is neither
We feel the status quo,
Contentment in the heart,
That's His love we know.

Thank You Lord for ups and downs
Lessons for the heart,
They keep us in Your loving care
Upon our daily path.

THE RIPPLES OF GOD'S GRACE

Take your thoughts
To a higher place,
Away from earth's trials
To the ripples of God's grace.

In the midst of your turmoil
The Saviour is by your side,
Lift your thoughts higher
He will help you to revive.

Open His Word for reassurance,
Be honest with yourself,
The ripples of God's grace
Will reach you to help.

There's nothing like God's grace,
A pardon to receive,
It comes hand in hand with mercy
If you will believe.

The gentle ripples of God's grace
Will reach you to the core,
To cleanse you inside out
Like the tide to the shore.

HOLY SPIRIT'S WHISPERS

The Holy Spirit's whispers
Come through His love for all,
So precious and sweet
To those who hear His call.

His whispers come softly
To soothe and heal,
He mends the broken hearted,
When in prayer they kneel.

He will pour His balm
So tenderly over you,
His sparkling living waters
Will make your heart brand new.

The Holy Spirit's whispers
Are such pure love,
Sent from the Saviour
From His Throne above.

HEALING WATERS

No ills can survive,
All wounds are soothed,
In His healing waters
Where the Spirit renews.

No hurt can survive
His healing waters will heal,
No scar so deep
That His love cannot remove.

All scars will disappear
In His healing balm,
A fragrance so sweet
Brings His peace and calm.

Healing waters refresh
And bathe the wounds of life,
Washing them away
In His streams of Light.

His peace will come
As you confess in trust and faith,
Healing waters of His balm
Remove your hurts without a trace.

THE SPIRIT'S BALM

The Spirit's balm Lord
Runs over my wounds,
He takes the years of hurt
Giving my heart room.

The Spirit's balm is moisture
Like cool summer rain,
It refreshes and restores
So I can live again.

The Spirit's balm is sent
With His tender loving care,
For every open heart
Who invites Him there.

His balm will come
When asked in heartfelt prayer,
A washing of the Spirit
Because He lingers there.

His balm is sweet and pure,
Because it comes from God,
So precious and sacred
Is the make-up of His love.

HIS WAYS ARE PERFECT...
TRUST AND RECEIVE...

"God is the one who has prepared us for this change, and he gave us his Spirit as the guarantee of all that he has in store for us."

2 Corinthians 5 : 5

HIS REASONS

The Lord has His reasons
For the path He plans for us,
We can rely on Him
And use our faith and trust.

They may not be our choice
Or the plans we made,
But the Lord has His reasons
For us to trust and obey.

Our path maybe steep
And the destination unknown,
The Lord has His reasons,
The way will be shown.

The Lord has His reasons
Why our faith comes to the test,
That's our learning time,
He's there to give us rest.

His way is perfect,
A lesson we may need,
But the Lord has His reasons
He will help us to succeed.

KEEPER OF MY SOUL

The precious Holy Spirit,
Keeper of my soul,
So sacred and pure,
He makes me feel whole.

He comes to live within
To shield me in His care,
He comforts and soothes me
While He abides there.

He prompts my heart to act
And refreshes my thoughts,
He gives me strength to rise above
The challenges I've fought.

His touch leaves me in awe,
The way God's love He's shown,
Because of You Holy Spirit,
My trust and faith have grown.

He comes with living waters
That wash me clean,
Precious Holy Spirit,
You show the Lord to me.

Precious Holy Spirit,
Jesus gave You to me,
Keeper of my soul
For all eternity.

RESTORE ME LORD

Restore me Lord
With compassion and care,
To be kind and thoughtful
Because Your commands You shared.

Forgive me when
I fall short some days,
My own wants and desires
Block the way.

Prompt me Holy Spirit
To look to You,
Finding solace and peace
All day through.

I ask for Your forgiveness
When all is said and done,
Restore me Lord
So I can overcome.

Restore me Lord
For the healing I need,
Pour Your soothing balm
Over all my needs.

WASHED BY THE SPIRIT

Being washed by His Spirit,
Your soul sparkles and shines,
You will feel complete
In His joy divine.

No words can explain
The Baptism of Christ's love,
When washed by His Spirit
Your life will open up.

His heart felt love awakes
His Spirit inside of you,
An enlightenment so real
Will make you feel brand new.

Feeling clean on the inside
Is like lightening in the sky,
A power so real
Your life will come alive.

RENEW MY STRENGTH

This I ask Father
For the challenges I face,
Renew my strength
In Your mercy and grace.

I care for my fellow man
For a lost soul to be saved,
I pray for the Spirit to heal them,
So they will know Your saving grace.

Renew my strength Lord
For the challenges that come my way,
Remind me to keep Your counsel
And to hear what You say.

I need You every day Lord,
In everything I do,
Renew my strength Lord
To see the glory in You.

BATHE YOUR SORROWS

Bathe your sorrows
With the Saviour's balm,
He will tenderly soothe you
In His loving arms.

Your troubles will soon fade away
When you give them to Him,
He will bathe your sorrows
To restore you within.

His Spirit will calm you
Because you used your faith
To leave your sorrows
At His Throne of Grace.

Though your heart feels heavy
And your spirit low,
The Lord will bathe your sorrows
So you can let them go!

Bathe your sorrows
In the Saviour's love,
You are His son or daughter,
He will never give you up!

ANCHOR YOUR LIFE…
IN HIS LOVE…

"…Whoever loves me will obey my teaching. My
Father will love him, and my Father and I
will come to him and live with him."

John 14 : 23

VICTORY IN THE SPIRIT

There's victory in the Spirit
When you claim help in the Saviour's Name,
There's no other way to overcome
Challenges that come your way.

You only have to ask
For help at hand,
Tell the Spirit what's on your mind,
He truly understands.

He will lay on your heart
Because you called your trust and faith,
His living waters will cleanse you
With soothing balm, He'll fill that place.

There's victory in the Spirit
When your peace is put to the test,
Call upon His help,
He will come with Spirit rest.

PRESS INTO THE SAVIOUR

Press into His power
When your world seems to dim,
Draw on your faith,
Keep your eyes on Him.

Pray so you can overcome
The darkest hour,
Ask Him to lift you above
To His light and power.

The deepest wound
He can wipe away,
Press into His love
With your trust and faith.

He will come to rescue
With a plan of His own,
He will fill your heart
Because it is His home.

Step into His light
For everything you need,
Press into His arms
Because you are His Holy Seed.

Press into His light,
It will never dim,
Talk to The Saviour,
You are His everything.

REFRESH MY HEART

Refresh my heart Lord
To fill it with Your light,
When I hear You talk to me
Everything is all right.

Cleanse it of impurities,
Heal it with Your balm,
Refresh my heart Lord,
Restore my peace and calm.

I long for a better world
That only You can transpire,
Refresh my heart Lord,
To lift my hopes higher.

Refresh my heart Lord
For that first love to impose
A commitment to repent
So your love can surely flow.

LIFE WEAVES A JOURNEY

Our lives weave a journey
With choices to make,
Each dawn brings a new day
But the Saviour stays the same.

There are many different challenges
In His plan that take place,
But we can walk with God
Through His mercy and grace.

We can follow His prompts,
He will help with the load,
You can walk in His light
That the Spirit will show.

Our lives weave a journey,
We have a destiny,
Call on the Saviour
He will supply the strength we need.

Our lives weave a journey
But the Lord has gone before,
Take everything to the Saviour
Because it's you He adores!

I CAN'T LIVE WITHOUT YOU

I need You with me always,
No matter where I am Lord,
You give Your loving care,
It's You I adore.

You're my refuge and my rock
In my daily life,
I can't live without You Lord,
I need You by my side.

You keep me safe in calm and storm
And share my happy or sad,
I believe You are with me,
That makes me glad.

When there's no one to talk to
You are always there,
I can't live without You Lord,
My all You will bear.

The Almighty Trinity,
Father, Son and Holy Ghost,
Thank You for saving me,
My precious Heavenly Hosts.

GOD'S HELP TODAY

I saw through my challenge,
I asked for God's help today,
So I could rise above
The fear that came my way.

I trusted that He would answer
My heartfelt call,
I prayed He would show me
A way out of it all.

When there's a shadow on my path
That just won't pass away,
I ask the Spirit to give me
His peace and calm today.

I will draw on my trust and faith
To rise above it all,
I know God's help will come
To answer my call.

AWAKEN MY SPIRIT

Awaken my spirit
With Your flame of love,
Through the Holy Spirit
Who came down from above.

Awaken my love
As each dawn breaks,
So I can give it out
Through my precious faith.

I love You more than anything
My heart tells me so,
Awaken my spirit
So Your love can flow.

Awaken my spirit Lord
With Your Holy Flame,
You will change me on the inside,
I will never be the same.

CALL ON THE SAVIOUR

Our comfort is the Saviour
No matter how we feel,
When we ask in heartfelt prayer
His love will be revealed.

In Him we have comfort
If we call Him to our side,
He will calm anxious moments
When in Him we confide.

Call on the Saviour
For every challenge of life,
As promised in His Word
He will not leave our side.

Nothing is ever lost,
Read His Word today,
Call on the Saviour
He will pave the way.

GOD'S PARADISE

Lord, You told of Your Paradise
And our Heavenly home,
That is ours if we believe,
Your salvation can be our own.

You told of Your wisdom
And knowledge centuries ago,
You made "Fishers of Men"
And told of the seeds we could sow.

You told of Your Heaven
And the wonders that await,
You told of Your glory,
How our sins You would take.

Your Paradise awaits
As Your Word tells us so,
Where mankind will kneel
At the Seat of Your Throne.

THANK HIS SPIRIT

Give thanks to His Spirit
So faithful and true,
He comes to comfort
To heal and console you.

He brings the love of the risen Lord
With grace and mercy every time,
It's you He adores,
His peace and rest you will find.

Though your path shows joy and pain
Give thanks to the Spirit,
His help you can claim
For you to get through it.

Call on the Holy Spirit
With thanks in your soul,
His help will come upon you
Like a soothing waterfall.

BORN AGAIN

Born again in You Lord,
I crave for every soul
To hear Your message of salvation,
To receive a Crown of Gold.

To turn from earth's ways
Of worry and doubts,
To welcome the Holy Spirit
Is what being born again is about.

We can rise above our fears
And own His peace and calm,
His strength will sustain us,
We only have to ask.

We can be free of guilt and shame
When we accept the King of Kings,
Being born again
Will change our heart within.

A light will shine inside,
We just have to learn His ways,
The Spirit will show us how,
He will teach us how to pray.

ACKNOWLEDGE GOD

Acknowledge God every day
As the new dawn awakes,
Time to start your chores
He will walk with you today.

His creation is all around us,
Everything we see,
Acknowledge God today
And His love we can receive.

His realm lays above,
But open hearts can receive
The gift of the Holy Spirit
For all who believe.

Acknowledge God as the Eternal Father,
Wonderful Counsellor, Prince of Peace,
Through His power and glory
His mercy and grace you can receive.

Acknowledge God in all you do,
You will walk in His light,
Acknowledge God and believe,
You will receive a Crown of Life.

PART THREE

"But when the kindness and love of God our Saviour was revealed, he saved us. It was not because of any good deeds that we ourselves had done, but because of his own mercy that he saved us, through the Holy Spirit, who gives us new birth and new life by washing us."

Titus 3 : 4 - 5

LIVING WATERS

OUR SHEPHERD...
WILL LEAD US...

"He lets me rest in fields of green grass
and leads me to quiet pools of fresh water."

Psalm 23 : 2

CALL GOD INTO YOUR LIFE

Call God into your life
For peace within,
Be sure your journey
Will take you closer to Him.

The bond between you
Will grow and grow
As the Holy Spirit whispers
His ways for you to know.

He will help you overcome
The weaknesses you feel,
Your prayer life renewed
As His life in you reveals.

Call God into your life
A revelation will take place,
Call on Him today
To receive His mercy and grace.

Call God into your life
Call on Him today,
No earthly joy can match
The blessings of God's ways.

FLOWING STREAMS

When words flow from my heart
In a constant stream,
Such a blessing I feel,
My pouring pen I need.

Flowing streams of strength
Just when I need them most,
I only have to ask
To receive from my Heavenly Host.

Flowing streams sparkle and shine
In Your light full of love,
A never ending supply,
From the Lord above.

Your Holy Spirit whispers
Your Words to me,
I write them down
In trust that You I please.

Flowing streams so healing
Can erase my doubts and fears,
In trust and faith I see
Flowing streams that bring You near.

I PRAY TO YOU LORD

I talk to You Father
Throughout my day,
Your joy I know,
My trust in You displayed.

I call for Your direction
To lead me on,
I pray Your care over me
All the day long.

I pray for special needs
In my family's affairs,
I pray Your will be done
Because You are beyond compare.

I pray for Your knowledge,
And wisdom to my mind,
Teach me Your ways Lord
So contentment I can find.

BAPTISM OF LOVE

The washing of the Spirit
Will cleanse you through and through,
If you open your heart to God
He will come to you.

A baptism of love
To thrill your soul,
A surrender of your heart
Will surely unfold.

His tender loving care
Will pour over you,
When you pray in earnest
He will honour you.

He knows your cares
And the concerns in your heart,
He will lead you gently
Down your life's path.

He will never leave you
Even though some days you despair,
He will cleanse you in the spirit,
You will know He is there.

In your baptism of love
You will rise in trust and faith,
Your God revelation revealing
His eternal mercy and grace!

BUILD ON YOUR FAITH

When you accept Christ Jesus into your heart,
He will supply your needs,
The Spirit will abide in you,
You will know tranquility.

You can build on your faith
To keep a happy heart,
Your strength will grow
As you walk His path.

A path of discipline
To stand apart from the world,
A path of compassion and love
As His Word tells.

You wear His Name,
It is divinely betrothed,
You inherit His Kingdom
Father, Son and Holy Ghost.

Build on your faith every day,
In prayer and reading His Word,
A power beyond your understanding
Because you, He came to serve.

THE SPIRIT BRINGS YOU NEAR LORD

The Spirit brings You near Lord
Because You gave Him to us,
To comfort, guide and protect
By showing us Your love.

He brings Your love so tenderly
With the touch of His hand,
The thrill many know
But don't really understand.

No words can explain
The wonder of His touch,
He brings You near Lord
With Your peace and love.

Like healing, flowing waters
With a full moon at night,
The Spirit brings You near Lord
For each open heart's delight.

LIVING WATERS

LIVING WATERS

THE HOLY SPIRIT…
WASHES US CLEAN…

"I will sprinkle clean water on you and make you clean…"

Ezekiel 36 : 25

WATERS THAT SPARKLE AND SHINE

Through the Saviour's Holy Spirit
Waters will sparkle and shine,
Daily He comes to me
Into this heart of mine.

Refreshing and restoring
His love will overflow,
Fountains of waters sparkle and shine
Where streams of glory flow.

Through His grace and mercy
Living waters offer life,
Eternal joy forever
In His glorious light.

Yes, living waters sparkle and shine
Like nothing we've ever seen,
In the Saviour's realm above
Where we will be received.

CALL ON THE SPIRIT

Call on the Spirit,
Holy and Divine,
One of The Trinity,
He will make your heart shine.

He can touch your soul,
He is majesty and grace,
Call on the Spirit,
You, He will embrace.

Call on the Spirit
For He is love itself,
Sent by the Saviour
To reveal Himself.

He brings the love of God
Into open hearts,
He shines His light within
So you can make a new start.

Call on the Spirit,
Great Comforter, Healer and Help,
Divine intervention,
His presence surely felt.

Call on the Spirit,
Eternal is His love,
Call on the Spirit
Sent down from above.

YOUR GREAT MAGNITUDE

Loving You; Your Spirit comes near
In great magnitude,
You are the Great Helper and Healer
Who draws me close to You.

Loving You; I feel You speak to me,
Your prompts come to mind,
Because of Your great magnitude,
Your answers I want to find.

Loving You; I can call on You,
My armour and my strength,
Fighting the battles before me
So I can receive Your calm and peace.

Loving You; Your great magnitude,
I need not doubt Your power,
I trust You are with me
Each and every hour.

RIGHT THE WRONG

Right the wrong in my life Lord,
Help me to see
How I can rectify
The changes I need.

Help me look at life
With a positive attitude,
To see the good in people,
I have the power to choose.

Only You can give me strength
To face each day that dawns,
Help me to right the wrong
When I'm feeling weary and worn.

Forgive me Lord when I criticize,
Remind me that's not Your way,
Help me to have a happy heart
To enjoy Your glorious day.

Right the wrong in me Lord
That only You can do,
Bring my heart gladness
Adoring only You!

ALL THINGS BRAND NEW

When you accept the Saviour
You will be washed clean,
His Spirit comes to live with you,
Now God's gift you have received.

A feeling of amazement
Will fill your soul,
No words can describe
Why you now feel "whole".

All things are brand new,
You see in a different light,
Your soul is now pure
Because God has made you right.

All things are renewed,
His blessings you now see,
He made you in His image,
Receive, now you have "believed".

A transformation so real,
Your ways He will change,
All things brand new,
Words just can't explain!

A VESSEL FOR JESUS

Be a vessel for Jesus,
Filled to the brim,
Forever overflowing
With love from Him.

A love so divine
That nothing can compare,
The heart knows eternal love
Because He lives there.

Be a vessel for Jesus
Filled with compassion and care,
Served by a loving heart
That honestly knows He is there.

Be a vessel of pure light
On the stormy seas of life,
Bringing His calm and peace
To change wrong to right.

Be a vessel for Jesus,
He needs you desperately,
To show His beloved
How He set you free.

PART FOUR

"Now my heart is troubled – and what shall I say? Shall I say, "Father, do not let this hour come upon me"? But that is why I came – so that I might go through this hour of suffering. Father, bring glory to your name!" Then a voice spoke from heaven, "I have brought glory to it, and I will do so again."

John 12 : 27 - 28

THE LAMB OF GOD...
SUFFERED FOR OUR SALVATION...

"They put a purple robe on Jesus, made a crown out of thorny branches, and put it on his head. Then they began to salute him: "Long live the King of the Jews!" They beat him over the head with a stick, spat on him, fell on their knees, and bowed down to him. When they had finished making fun of him, they took off the purple robe and put his own clothes back on him. Then they led him out to crucify him."

Mark 15 : 17 - 20

PROPHECY REVEALED

The Saviour born in the Stable
Would be God's sacrifice,
Prophesied centuries ago,
The Lamb would give His life.

The Lord called them together,
All was prepared,
The night before Calvary,
A sacred meal they shared.

Prophecy was revealed
In the Upper Room that night,
One would betray
The world's Shining Light.

This would be their last meal
Before the Trial to come,
One would betray, one would deny
God's only Holy Son.

A pouch of silver to gain,
And a kiss would be the sign,
A Disciple would betray
The Lord God Divine.

Jesus of Nazareth, Almighty God,
The Everlasting Father, Prince of Peace,
Prophecy revealed
He will bring us to our knees!

FATHER OF MANKIND

A power so great can create the world
And be the Eternal Light,
He entered the womb of a gentle soul
To be the Father of mankind.

His Father in Heaven sent Him
To save all people from sin,
He is the Lamb of God,
With a message to believe in Him.

He was nailed and died on a wooden Cross,
Stained with His blood Divine,
He took the weight of the world,
The Father of mankind.

He was buried in a tomb
But on the Third day rose to life,
God raised His precious Son,
The Father of mankind.

A priceless mission
He gave for you and I
Because He took the Cross,
You can have a Crown of Life.

The precious Lord Jesus,
King of Kings, the Lord Divine,
Saviour of the world,
Son of God, Father of mankind.

FILL ME WITH GOODNESS

Fill me with goodness Lord,
The kind Your Spirit sends,
Keep my heart open
With Your love without end.

I claim Your righteousness
And protection over me,
I believe in Your truth
To set me free.

I receive Your grace and mercy
That came from Calvary,
From Your death on the Cross,
You rose to victory.

You came for this one purpose,
To save mankind from sin,
Fill me with Your goodness Lord
Where Your Spirit lives within.

I thank You dear Saviour,
Lay on my heart,
Thank You Lord Jesus
How precious You are!

THREE DAYS LATER...
HE WILL RISE...

"He reflects the brightness of God's glory and is
the exact likeness of God's own being, sustaining
the universe with his powerful word. After
achieving forgiveness for the sins of mankind,
he sat down in heaven at the right side
of God, the Supreme Power."

Hebrews 1 : 3

HE LED BY EXAMPLE

He came to earth from Heaven
To fulfill His Father's plan,
A young boy from Nazareth
Grew into a man.

He led by example
To His Chosen few,
The parables He told them
Would forever be the truth.

A thirty year journey
From the Manger to the Cross,
For our salvation and redemption
His life would be the cost.

Sweet victory was His
As He rose from the grave,
Through His Father's great glory
Now forgiveness was attained.

Yes, He led by example
Our Teacher and Lord,
He led by example,
The Saviour we adore!

THE SYMBOL OF THE CROSS

There is no other symbol
That marks a sacrifice,
Given for the world
By our precious Lord Jesus Christ.

Sacred without words,
A symbol for life,
Why the Saviour took the Cross
For you and I.

It's meaning so powerful,
The agony so real,
A cup He couldn't refuse
So the scriptures would be fulfilled.

A symbol of forgiveness,
A symbol so divine,
That bought Redemption
With His blood instead of mine.

Yes, the symbol of the Cross
Stands for sacrifice and victory,
His blood shed for the world
So we can have Eternity.

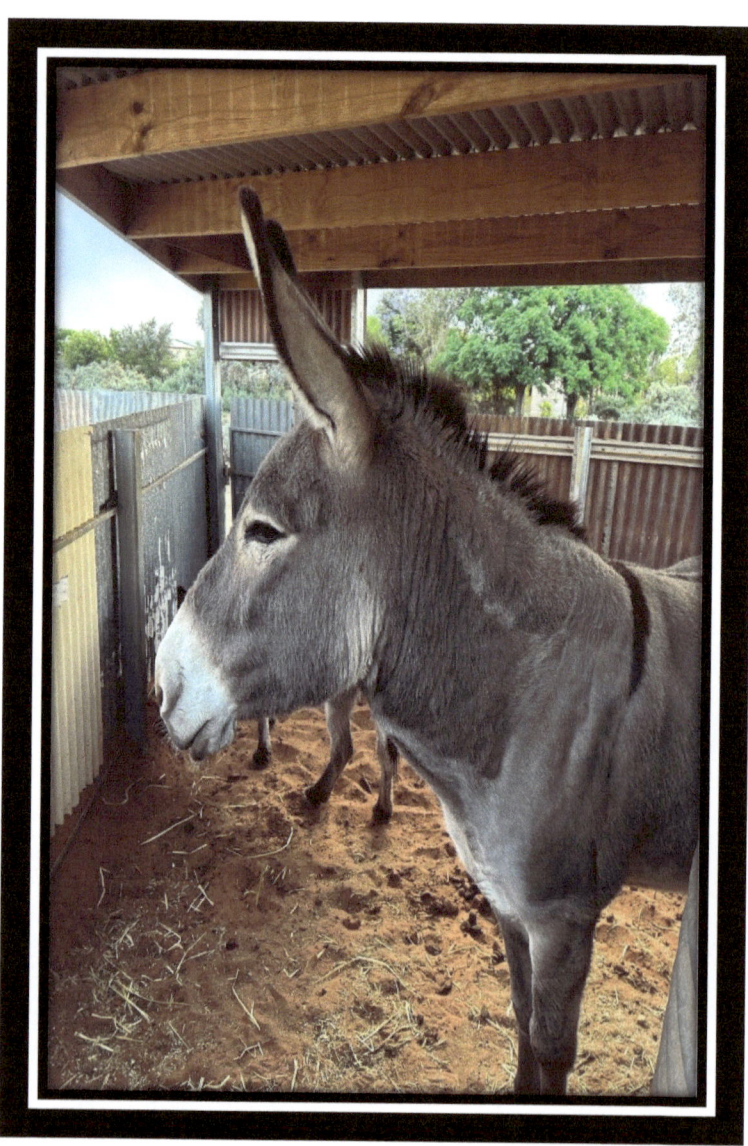

CHRIST'S BIRTH BROUGHT GREAT...
JOY, PEACE AND HOPE...

"The angel said to her, "Don't be afraid, Mary; God has been gracious to you. You will become pregnant and give birth to a son, and you will name him Jesus. He will be great and will be called the Son of the Most High God."...

Luke 1 : 30 - 32

FIRST CHRISTMAS MORN

Dawn on Christmas Day,
My heart fills with love,
Mankind comes together
For the birth of God's only Son.

A celebration so Holy
For Christ the Lord,
Born in a stable,
The first Christmas morn.

The Star in the East
Shone brightly above,
Angels from Heaven
Sang of His love.

The first Christmas morn
Brings peace on earth indeed,
So we can worship the Lord
In all His majesty!

IN AWE SHE HELD HIM

In awe she held Him,
Born that Holy Night,
In wonder and majesty,
The Star above shone bright.

Heavenly angels rejoiced
In unison they sang,
Glory to the Lord,
He is the Holy Lamb.

In awe she held Him,
The newborn Holy Christ,
Wrapped in swaddling clothes,
The world's Shining Light.

Now golden dawn awakes,
Orange sweeps the sky,
Glory fills the stable,
God's precious Son arrived.

In awe she held Him;
Born the King of Kings,
He lives forever more,
Salvation to the world He brings!

WHAT JOY, WHAT JOY

Glad tidings rang out
On that Holy Night,
The angels appeared to the shepherds,
The night sky shone bright.

The Messiah born in Bethlehem,
Born this very night,
The Star stops overhead,
What joy, what joy tonight.

Inside the humble stable,
The King of Kings is born,
Mary held God's Son,
All glory to the Lord.

Glad tidings to the world,
The Christ Child born tonight,
Our Redeemer has arrived
What joy, what joy tonight!

TRUTH AND GRACE HIS STRONGHOLD

Thank You Father
For that Holy Night,
The Saviour arrived
To be our Shining Light.

He left Your side in Glory
To be the Saviour of the world,
Truth and grace His stronghold,
His message He would tell.

Conceived by the Holy Spirit
Mary delivered the Son of God,
So humbly in the stable,
Who the world would lean upon.

Obedient servants, Mary and Joseph
What a privilege to bear,
They raised God's precious Son,
Entrusted in their care.

Truth and grace His stronghold,
Ours to live a righteous life,
In the presence of the Father,
Our Lord and Saviour, Jesus Christ.

ALSO BY CLAIRE GROSE

  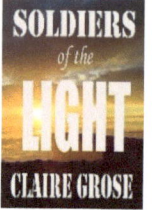

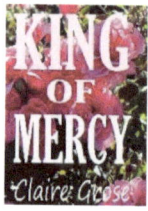  

ABOUT THE AUTHOR

Claire worked as a Government Public Servant in the Lands Department, Adelaide, South Australia until she married and became a mother of two boys.

She later returned to the work force during which time she gained a "Living Hope" Phone Counselling certificate which influenced her need to help others.

Through this and personal experience she found herself inspired by God's love to put pen to paper.

PHOTO CREDITS

COVER PHOTO: Mawson Lakes Fountain; S.A. – Claire Grose

Page 2: Mawson Lakes Fountain; S.A. - Claire Grose
Page 12: Bird Bath; S.A. – Claire Grose
Page 24: Montville Rainforest; Qld – Claire Grose
Page 31: Sturt's Desert Pea; NSW. – Jane and Scott
Page 39: Windchime; S.A. – Lynne
Page 47: Mawson Lakes Walkway; S.A. - Claire Grose
Page 55: Fremont Park Duck Pond; S.A. – Claire Grose
Page 70: Sheep, Barossa Valley; S.A. – Claire Grose
Page 78: Blake's Crossing Fountain; S.A – Claire Grose
Page 87: Salisbury Uniting Church Cross; S.A – Claire Grose
Page 92: Salisbury Uniting Church Cross; S.A – Claire Grose
Page 96: Donkey and Colt; NSW – Jane and Scott

LIVING WATERS

www.ingramcontent.com/pod-product-compliance
Lightning Source LLC
Chambersburg PA
CBHW042043290426
44109CB00001B/15